P9-CRM-054

GEORGE and ROBERT STEPHENSON, father and son, are best known for their steam locomotive, the *Rocket*, and for the foundation of today's system of rail transport; in fact, they achieved far more than this. The Stockton and Darlington line and the Manchester and Liverpool line, the first passenger line in the world, were two of George's greatest feats of engineering. Robert built the famous Britannia tubular steel bridge in Wales, the Victoria Bridge in Canada, and railways from the London and Birmingham to the Egyptian State Railway between Alexandria and Cairo. Together they built over three hundred miles of railway, and revolutionized passenger and goods transport in Britain. The Victorian age was one of great social and industrial progress; George and Robert Stephenson were giants of that age.

In this fascinating account of the Stephensons' life and work, appealing to historian and scientist alike, Colin Dorman traces their remarkable progress over the eighty years between father's birth and son's death, from the poverty of George's youth to Robert's eventual prosperity. The book is clearly written, and technical terms are explained in the comprehensive glossary. There are more than fifty illustrations, a date chart, reading list, and index.

COLIN CRESSWELL DORMAN was born at Smethwick, Staffordshire, in 1911, and his interest in railways and railway history was first aroused as a pupil at King Edward's School, Birmingham. Since that time he has travelled on railways all over the world and has written a number of books of which *The London and North Western Railway* and *the Liverpool Railway Scene* have also been published by Wayland Publishers.

The Stephenson family. *Standing, left to right* Robert and Mabel
Stephenson, George Stephenson's parents; George Stephenson
and his son Robert. *Sitting* Fanny Henderson, George's first wife,
holding their daughter; Elizabeth Hindmarsh, George's second
wife.

Pioneers of Science and Discovery

The Stephensons and Steam Railways

C. C. Dorman

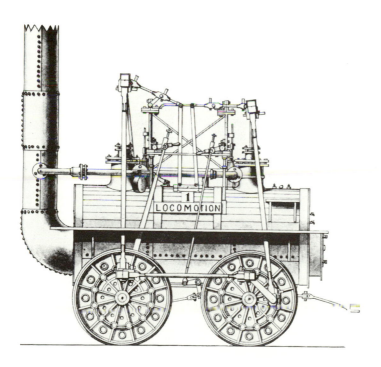

Other Books in this Series

SBN 85078 223 6
Copyright © 1975 by C. C. Dorman
First published in 1975 by
Wayland Publishers Limited
49 Lansdowne Place, Hove, East Sussex BN3 1HF
Second impression 1977
Third impression 1980
Printed and bound in Great Britain
at The Pitman Press, Bath

Contents

List of Illustrations

Introduction

George and Robert Stephenson were true pioneers. With little education, and in poor conditions, they worked with their own hands to make themselves known in the world of engineering. When they had done this, they put their own ideas into action and set about building the first ever steam railway in the world. Britain's present railway system is the direct result of their life and work.

Before the Stephensons, transport in Britain was mainly limited to horse-drawn barges on canals, for heavy goods, and horse-drawn carriages on roads, for passengers. Yet railways had been in use for centuries, ever since the days of the Roman Empire. Gradually the tracks were developed, from wooden roads with metal plates nailed to them, to iron rails specially shaped to fit the wheels of the waggons. These tracks were called tramways. The waggons were drawn up-hill by horses, and ran back down again under their own weight. This system was still in use well into the nineteenth century.

Opposite top The first horse-drawn carriage to run on rails. *Bottom* An early system of transporting coal.
Below left A detail of the first tramway, showing the flanged metal rail. *Right* A mine truck of the sixteenth century.

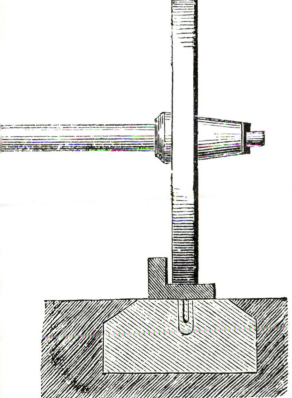

The idea of a machine driven by steam was also a very old one. In ancient Greece, almost two thousand years ago, Hero of Alexandria had built a hollow metal ball with two bent pipes, one on either side. When this sphere was filled with steam from a boiler the steam escaped through the pipes, and the ball turned. Yet it was not until much later that the possibilities of steam power were fully understood. In the seventeenth century a steam driven pumping engine was built by Thomas Savery (1650?–1715), and his idea was later improved by Thomas Newcomen (1663 – 1729). But so far steam engines were not very efficient, because they wasted so much heat.

James Watt (1736 – 1819) was the first man to make a really efficient steam engine, by using all the extra heat to make the engine work harder. But he did not see that it could be made to move itself, rather than just pump water or lift heavy weights. The first moving steam engine was built by a Frenchman, Joseph Cugnot (1725 – 1804) in 1769. It did not use rails, and when Cugnot drove it through the streets of Paris it overturned and crashed. It was then locked up for safety!

Richard Trevithick (1771 – 1833), a Cornishman, did better when in 1804 he tried out the first real

Right A model of Hero's aeolipile, a machine which showed the power of steam under pressure.

Below Joseph Cugnot's steam engine of 1769.

railway steam engine. Unfortunately the track was not strong enough, and it broke under the weight of the engine and its waggons; but Trevithick was nearly there. In 1809 he brought to London his new engine, the *Catch-me-who-can*, and it ran successfully around a circular track pulling a carriage full of amazed spectators. The steam railway had been born; George and Robert Stephenson took it and made it into a transport revolution.

The railways played a major part in the improvement of social conditions in the nineteenth century. They made it possible for the first time for everyone to travel about the country, to new jobs and new homes. Many an able man spent all his life in one job, in one place, before the railway opened the whole country to his ambitions. We should remember that the men who grew up with the Stephensons had never known anything but the horse for work and travel. These same men lived to see express trains hurtling along at sixty miles per hour.

For this reason alone the Stephensons were major figures in the development of the thrusting Victorian age. Their railways were the vital arteries through which it lived and thrived. They were responsible for much of its splendour, not only with their magnificent bridges and viaducts but also with their stations. Many of these, with their high glass roofs, were sometimes compared to temples. Temples that is, to the God of Progress. It was the faith and vision of the Stephensons which made all this possible.

We have conquered the air, and we can now travel faster than sound, but surely no step of man's progress can ever be compared with that first leap forward from the horse to the express train. The story of the Stephensons is the story of that leap.

Richard Trevithick's *Catch-me-who-can* running at Euston Square in 1809.

13

1 *Early Years*

Wylam on the Tyne, home of Robert and Mabel Stephenson.

The mining village of Wylam lies on the north bank of the River Tyne, about eight miles west of Newcastle. At the end of the eighteenth century it was part of the estate of Christopher Blackett, a local land and colliery owner who was also the proprietor of the Globe newspaper. It was here that Robert and Mabel Stephenson lived, in a humble two-storied dwelling known as High Street House. This couple were George Stephenson's father and mother.

Robert Stephenson, "Owd Bob" as the neighbours called him, was the son of a Scot who took work in England as a gentleman's servant. His wife, Mabel, was the daughter of Robert Carr, a dyer from Ovingham. She was, it is said, of delicate health, but this is surely disproved by her bringing up a family of six children. She managed to do all this on her husband's wage of twelve shillings per week. This was what Owd Bob earned for looking after the winding engine at the Wylam colliery.

For some time after their marriage they had lived at Walbottle, near the river Tyne, but soon moved to High Street House where their children were born. It must have been a noisy home, for three other miner's families also lived there. The Stephenson family bible contains the following entries:

James Stephenson	born 4th March, 1779
George Stephenson	born 9th June, 1781
Eleanor Stephenson	born 16th April, 1784
Robert Stephenson	born 10th March, 1788
John Stephenson	born 4th November, 1789
Ann Stephenson	born 19th July, 1792

Times were hard. There was no money to spare for education and because of this none of the children received any schooling.

The interior of High Street House at Wylam, where George Stephenson was born.

Owd Bob was a great favourite in the village, particularly with the children. The stories he told them were greatly enjoyed. He was also something of an animal lover, and he had many tame pets. These were as happy sitting by his engine fire at the colliery as were the boys and girls listening to his stories. His children, although victims of the poor conditions, were members of a loving and devoted family. George

Opposite Outside High Street House, showing the waggon way running by the front door.

Below This model locomotive is said to have been the first engine ever built by George Stephenson, when he was a boy.

developed a keen sense of responsibility early on in life. As one of the older members of the family he did his share of household duties and of looking after the youngsters. Also, like many of later generations, he took Owd Bob's dinner to his place of work. This meant walking alongside the wooden-railed tram road, over which the coal waggons were dragged by horses. This waggon way was the first on which a locomotive was tried out; but such a thought cannot possibly have occurred to George or his father at the time.

When George Stephenson was about eight years old his father's engine was dismantled, as it was worn out. Owd Bob had to look for another job. He eventually found one at the Dewley Burn colliery, as a fireman in charge of a steam engine. The family moved at once to Dewley Burn. There they lived in a single-roomed cottage beside a stream. The pit at which Owd Bob worked was behind the cottage. George was now old enough to make his contribution to the family expenses, and he got his first regular job. This was with a widow named Grace Ainslie, who employed him as a cow-herd. He also had another job as gateman on the waggon way, at a wage of twopence a day. His duty was to see that the gates were barred at night after the last waggons had passed, and "his" cows had been shut up.

He had plenty of spare time for bird's nesting and other boyhood pursuits, and it was here that the budding engineer made his first attempts at modelling; his favourite hobby (the shape of things to come) was building clay engines. He would use string for the windings and reeds as steam pipes. Everything about engines was magic to him. His usual companion in this was a boy named Billy Thirlwall. Billy later became an engineer at a colliery near Alnwick, a post he held for thirty years.

As George grew older and stronger he was set to leading the plough horses, and to hoeing turnips and other farm work. For this he was paid fourpence a day. But he longed to do colliery work, and soon after this he joined his elder brother James at the Dewley Burn pit, as a "picker." This meant clearing the coal of stones, bricks, and other bits and pieces. Later he was given a better job as a gin driver at the Black Callerton colliery. Coal was brought up from the pit in buckets. Ropes were tied to the buckets and wound up on a drum; this drum was known as a "gin." A gin-horse was used to turn the drum. Round and round the horse went on its endless journey. Even then, George may well have thought of an engine to do the poor animal's work.

As with his father, wild life was of great interest to

Two kinds of pump. In the background is a horse-powered gin, in the foreground the more modern steam-driven pumps.

him. His love of wild birds grew, and remained with him all his life. One of his tame blackbirds would roost upon his bed head at night, and would spend the day playing in and around the cottage. He also built himself a rabbit hutch in the garden, and won some fame locally as a breeder.

After driving the gin at the Black Callerton pit he was taken on as his father's assistant, to help fire the engine at Dewley Burn colliery. George was never really happy unless he was working with engines. He was then fourteen years old and earned one shilling a day. This job as assistant fireman was really the first step he took towards realizing his ambition to become an engine-man, in charge of his own engine. Dewley Burn colliery was soon worked out, and eventually the pit was closed. George and Owd Bob were put out of work, and in those days there was none of the help which is now given to workmen who suffer such a blow.

2 Marriage and the Birth of Robert

After the Dewley Burn colliery was closed, Owd Bob and his family moved a few miles south to Jolly's Close, near Newburn. Owd Bob took a job at the Duke of Northumberland's pit, called "the Duke's Winning," and George started work at another pit, the "Mid Mill Winning," as a fireman. His wage was one shilling a day. He was then fifteen years old. When the

Newburn on the Tyne, near to the Stephensons' second home at Jolly's Close.

pit at Mid Mill was closed in its turn, George and his friend and workmate, Billy Coe, were sent to work the pumping engine at the Throckley Bridge pit. There his wages were raised to twelve shillings a week. He was very pleased. He was now earning a "man's wage." Tales about the wonderful steam engines built by Matthew Boulton (1728 – 1809) and James Watt (1736 – 1819) came to his ears; he wanted to get to know more about them. Already he knew all there was to know about Thomas Newcomen's pumping engine, built a hundred years earlier.

Soon afterwards Owd Bob was made fireman to a

Matthew Boulton and James Watt worked together to produce the first efficient steam pumping engines, such as the beam engine pictured here.

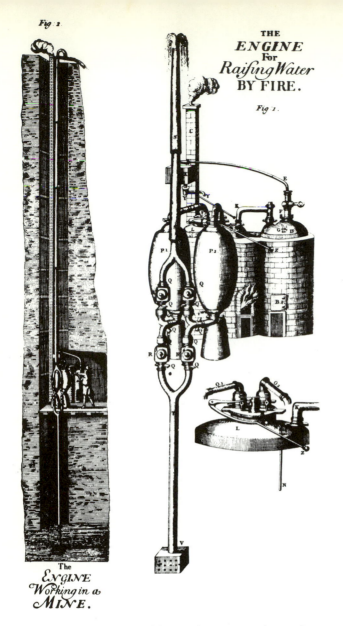

Fig. 2

THE
ENGINE
For
Raising Water
BY FIRE.

Fig. 1.

The
ENGINE
Working in a
MINE.

An early steam pumping engine shown working in a mine. It was this kind of engine that George Stephenson worked on as a plugman.

pumping engine erected by Robert Hawthorn (1796–1867), the Duke's engineer, at Newburn. George was appointed as his "plugman." This was a responsible job for a youngster of seventeen, and he was considered senior to his own father. He had to make sure that the engine was working efficiently. When the suction of the pump became poor, due to the lowering of the water level in the pit, the tube had to be plugged at the bottom of the shaft. He studied the engine

George Stephenson throwing the hammer. As well as being an athletic young man, he had plenty of courage, as the story on the next page tells.

carefully, taking it to pieces, and putting it together again in his spare time. In this way he got to know its working and its peculiarities very thoroughly indeed.

George, at eighteen, could still not read. He began to realize that if he was to make real progress in life, he would have to do something about it. He started going to night school, at first with a teacher named Robin Cowens, who ran an evening class for the sons of working men. The lessons cost him fourpence a week. Later he joined a class run by Andrew Robinson at Newburn. He was a hard-working pupil and his progress was rapid. It is strange to think of George starting school just at the age when most children today are leaving.

In a couple of years he was appointed brakesman at the Dolly pit. His job was to look after the winding machine at the head of the pit. For the sake of convenience he took lodgings at a small farm in the village. Here he met a girl named Frances Henderson, who was the servant at his lodgings.

It was at about this time that he had his first and only fight. He had quarrelled, over something quite petty, with a pit worker called Ned Nelson. To everyone's surprise, when the fight took place George won easily. This was an early indication of his physical courage, for he was no boxer. Yet he refused to be trampled on by the local bully, and he afterwards shook hands with his enemy. In later years his courage was often severely tried in other ways, and he showed equal bravery when dealing with the financial bullies of the big railway companies.

George Stephenson was now twenty-one and known to be an expert workman. He was as strong as he would ever be. As well as his job at the Dolly pit he did extra work emptying ships on the quayside, and repaired shoes and clocks for his neighbours in his spare time. His reading and writing were still improving. He also made his first attempts at inventing something of his own. He was unsuccessful. A self-reversing engine brake which he made proved an utter failure.

Soon a matter of great importance was arranged: his marriage to Frances Henderson. This became possible because he had received an offer to take over the winding engine at Willington Ballast Hill, on the River Tyne. This meant a higher wage. He took a cottage at Willington Quay, and with Fanny's help he furnished it, humbly but comfortably, in readiness for the great day. The wedding took place at Newburn Church on the 28th November, 1802. George's signature in the Church register is childishly simple, and because of the similarity of the writing he probably signed for Frances as well. After the ceremony the young couple spent the day at Owd Bob's. In the evening they left on a horse for their new home. The bride rode "pillion" behind her husband

Right   The marriage register of Newburn Church, showing George Stephenson's signature.

George Stephenson Bachelor & Frances Henderson,
Spinster both of this Parish were married in this
Church by Banns this twenty eighth Day of
November 1802 by me Thos Stee Curate
This marriage was solemnized between us
George Stephenson   Frances Henderson
In presence of us   Thos Thompson Edwd Nicholson

Below   After their wedding, George and his wife, Frances, rode home to Willington on horseback.

George Stephenson's first married home, at Willington Quay, on the river Tyne.

for the fifteen mile journey.

Thus began their married life, very humbly, but they were both full of hope. George was determined to improve their lot, and began to study the principles of mechanics. He used to sit with his books beside his young wife in the winter evenings. He amused himself by trying to invent a perpetual motion engine. He built a wooden wheel and studded the rim with glass tubes. These he filled with mercury, which poured down from one tube to the next as the wheel turned. Unfortunately, it stopped!

A frequent visitor to their home was William Fair-

The pit head at West Moor colliery.

bairn (1789–1874). William was at that time an engine apprentice at the Percy Main colliery. He later helped George's son, Robert, in the building of the Britannia bridge in Wales. He became President of the British Association*, and in 1869 was made Sir William Fairbairn.

It was while they were living at Willington Quay that Frances gave birth to their only son, on the 16th October, 1803. The young Robert soon became a great favourite with his father, and he was the source of much pleasure to the young couple. After three years at Willington, George was persuaded to leave for a similar job at the West Moor colliery, at Killingworth. He had not been long in this new job before he suffered the most dreadful personal blow of his life. Frances died of tuberculosis.

As a result, when he was offered a job at Montrose, in Scotland, he readily accepted. He was put in charge

*An association founded in 1831 to bring together important scientists and engineers.

of a Boulton and Watt engine. Leaving Robert in the care of the lady who had been housekeeping for him, George set off on foot for Montrose. He was well paid during the year he worked there and managed to save twenty-eight pounds before walking back again to Killingworth.

At home disaster awaited him, for Owd Bob had suffered a serious accident at work. He had been blinded. George quickly settled his father's mounting debts, and began to take care of him for his remaining years. As well as this he had to spend the rest of his savings in finding a militia man to take his place when he was called up for the great war which England was fighting against France. So his fortunes were at a low ebb at this time, and all his savings were gone.

Luckily his skill as an engineer was becoming well known, and he got extra work repairing worn-out pumping engines. His skill eventually led to his appointment, in 1812, as the engine-man at Killingworth High pit. His luck had changed.

Killingworth High pit, where George Stephenson started work in 1812 as an engine-man.

3 Blutcher and the Safety Lamp

Opposite top An engraving made in 1812 of John Blenkinsop's rack locomotive. The caption on the engraving describes the engine as "capable of moving one hundred tons at 3½ miles an hour on a level rail road."

Opposite below A photograph of William Hedley's *Wylam Dilly,* built in 1813. Like Blenkinsop's engine, the two cylinders were mounted vertically, at the rear of the boiler. The power was transmitted to the wheels through the mass of rods and levers mounted above the boiler.

George continued to be happy in his hobby of watch and clock repairing, and everyone in the neighbourhood took advantage of his services. The comfortable little home at Killingworth was filled with his small inventions, together with models of engines that he had made.

Because of his appointment as engineer to the Killingworth pit, George did not have to do much manual work. He became the proud owner of a gig, the sign of a man of some importance. His much loved Galloway mare was put out to grass, and he used to make working visits in the gig to the nearby collieries of the Killingworth field. It was at about this time that the steam locomotive and its possibilities began to obsess him. This marked the beginning of the career which was to make him one of the greatest self-made men in history. The fame of his successes with the Killingworth pit engines had spread far and wide; many leaders of industry in the North East knew him as "Geordie" Stephenson, the "engine doctor."

George Stephenson was now planning his first self-acting incline at Willington Quay. A few years before, a Leeds colliery-owner named John Blenkinsop had built an engine that successfully hauled thirty waggons for three miles in an hour. In the process it smashed most of the rails because of its own weight. Encouraged by the performance of the engine, Christopher Blackett of Wylam ordered a locomotive to work on a toothed driving wheel, upon a rack-rail; this rail was made to fit the teeth on the wheel. The locomotive had been tried out at Leeds, with an engine built by Thomas Waters of Gateshead. It was a cross between the earlier designs of Richard Trevithick and John Blenkinsop, and it turned out to be more awkward than both of them. It was taken to Wylam and mounted on a wooden frame with four pairs of wheels, but it refused to start. Waters became so angry that he mis-used the safety-valve and the engine blew up. Yet Mr. Blackett refused to be disheartened. His efforts were rewarded when a fourth engine worked well, in spurts. Unfortunately, the engine was so noisy that his driver had to be ordered to shut off steam whenever a person (or an animal) came into sight.

This was the engine Stephenson saw at work, and he thought he could improve upon it. He immediately started work on his first locomotive in one of the colliery workshops, but his tools were more suited to repairing pump-engines. After ten months of hard work using such spare time as he had from his normal job, he finally produced an engine. He christened it *Blutcher,* after the Prussian general who later fought with the Duke of Wellington (1769–1852) at the battle of Waterloo in 1815. Stephenson did not realize that he had spelled the name wrongly.

The locomotive was put on the rails at Killingworth on the 25th July, 1814. Its most prominent features were a huge boiler and a towering funnel. Despite this odd appearance the engine worked, and it successful-ly pulled the eight heavy test waggons up a slight slope at four miles per hour. *Blutcher* continued at work, and while doing so it settled a problem that had worried engineers from the beginning. This was the expected slipping of the smooth wheels on the smooth rails. As Stephenson had foreseen, with enough weight on the wheels, they would grip, and grip they did.

The *Blutcher* during its short life solved other problems. One was that the shriek of the steam es-caping from the cylinders terrified nearby cattle, and indeed, it must have been rather frightening. The other was that the loss of this steam made it impos-sible to keep up pressure in the boiler. Stephenson

Marshal Blucher, whose name George Stephenson took for his first locomotive. The Prussians were allies of Britain at the beginning of the nineteenth century, and Blucher achieved a notable victory over Napoleon at Laon, in France, in 1814. In the following year he played a part in the Duke of Wellington's victory at Waterloo.

began a series of experiments to cure these faults. Eventually he managed to turn the blast of steam from the cylinders into the chimney, thus solving the noise and pressure problems at a stroke. This was an important step in the development of the steam locomotive, and when he came to build his second engine, the *Wellington*, it was a factor in its favour. All of these improvements helped to ensure the future of the steam locomotive.

Mr. Bruce's school in Newcastle, where Robert Stephenson went from the age of twelve.

Now little Robert was growing up, and his training and education began to take up more and more of his father's time. The boy spent hours eagerly watching the little pump that had been set up at the Ochre Quarry, near his home, to keep it dry. As soon as he was old enough he was sent to school. George was determined that his son should not suffer the poor education that he himself had had to bear. He had saved one hundred pounds, in spite of the cost of caring for his father.

When Robert was twelve he was sent to Dr. Bruce's school in Newcastle. He rode there and back every day on a donkey which his father had bought. His fees were money well spent, for he did very well at school. As a result, his father's own education improved, too. At night the pair used to have long discussions on what Robert had been taught. For instance George learned, through his son, how to read plans without looking at the written instructions. This was to be very useful to him in later life.

As well as his work on steam locomotives, George Stephenson was involved in other projects. One in particular reached its climax at about this time, and caused a national scientific argument.

During his work on *Blutcher* he had invented a miner's safety lamp, designed to combat the ever-present danger of explosions of fire-damp—a kind of explosive gas found in coal mines. The Killingworth colliery had suffered from this danger. In 1806, when Stephenson was a brakesman there, ten men were killed in an explosion, and he was deeply affected. He vowed to do anything in his power to stop these dreadful accidents happening. A similar tragedy took place in 1809, when twelve more lives were lost, and at the neighbouring Felling pit, near Gateshead, there were no fewer than ninety casualties.

By 1815 Stephenson, though very busy with his locomotive interest, was still working on this problem of inflammable gas. He produced the first of three

safety lamps, which he tested at Killingworth. Showing great courage, he personally conducted experiments down the pit. Instead of lighting the fire-damp, the lamp kept going out, and Stephenson was disappointed with its performance. He made improvements to it in his own house, helped by his son, Robert. A second, and later a third lamp were built before George was satisfied. Then began an angry argument over the respective merits of Stephenson's "Geordie" lamp, as it became known, and Sir Humphry Davy's lamp.

Sir Humphry (1778 – 1829) had been awarded

When George Stephenson tested his safety lamp in the Killingworth pit he had to do it alone. The danger of an explosion of fire-damp was so great that his companions remained well out of harm's way.

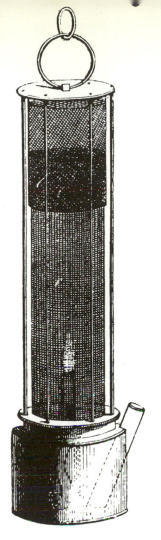

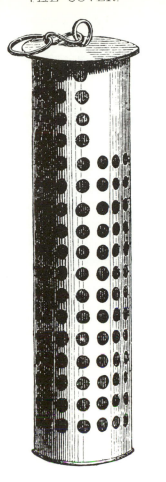

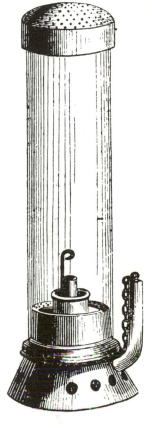

DAVY'S SAFETY-LAMP.

STEPHENSON'S SAFETY-LAMP.

Stephenson's safety lamp *(right)*, compared with Sir Humphry Davy's lamp *(left)*. Each lamp worked as well as the other, but Davy was given all the credit for the invention himself.

£2,000 as "inventor of the safety lamp." Quite unfairly George got only £100 for the work he had done. As a result, a local fund was launched, headed by Lord Ravensworth, a partner in the Killingworth colliery. His Lordship contributed one hundred guineas himself, and eventually the total sum collected reached £1,000. This was presented to the inventor at the Assembly rooms in Newcastle. He was, of course, very grateful for this generous gift, but the reward he most appreciated was an inscribed silver watch given to him by the miners, a token of their high regard for him. But who had really been the first man to invent the safety lamp? It seems that the inventions were "parallel." Both men arrived at the same destination, but by different routes. The £1,000 award was very useful when George later started his own locomotive works.

In 1819 George was asked by the Hetton Coal Company to build them a railway over a hilly eight miles from the Hetton colliery, in Durham, to the River Wear, near Sunderland. He was, and remained all through his life, convinced that steam engines were best suited to a level track. But the colliery company refused to spend vast sums on levelling the road, so he was forced to construct the line over the existing slopes. He did this by using stationary engines to haul the waggons up the hills.

While he was working on the Hetton railway George remarried, after fourteen years as a widower. His second wife was Elizabeth Hindmarsh, a farmer's daughter from Black Callerton. She was a kindly and affectionate woman, and loved Robert as though he were her own child. There can be no doubt that she contributed greatly to the happiness of both father and son.

Two years later the Hetton railway project was completed, and the line was opened on 18th November, 1822. The whole district treated the day as a holiday and swarmed round the track. Everyone stared in amazement as the engine, brought over from Killingworth, was coupled to seventeen waggons and stormed away at a steady four miles per hour. Surely it was the eighth wonder of the world!

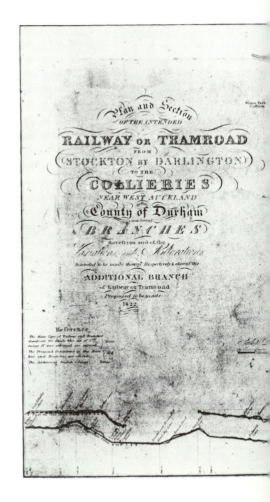

4 The Stockton and Darlington Railway

A map made in 1822 of the line from Stockton to Darlington, showing the extension of the line westwards to the collieries of Durham. This line was the first to use steam locomotives over its whole length.

In 1821 a group of wealthy men, headed by a businessman called Edward Pease (1767 – 1858), had obtained permission for a line between Stockton and Darlington. Stephenson, of course, heard about this, and was fascinated by the idea. With the help of Nicholas Wood, the head viewer at the Killingworth colliery, he arranged to meet Edward Pease in Darlington. At this meeting he asked to be considered for the post of engineer to the railway. Mr. Pease was

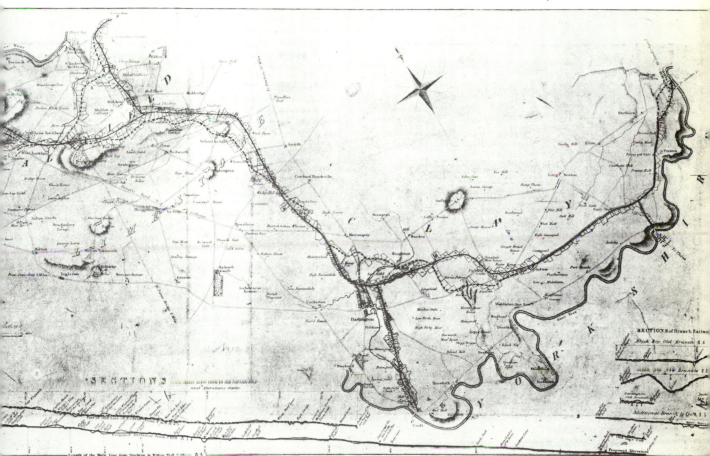

A share certificate for the Stockton and Darlington Railway, issued in 1823. Money paid by the shareholders was used to pay for the building of the line. If it turned out to be profitable, the shares would increase in value.

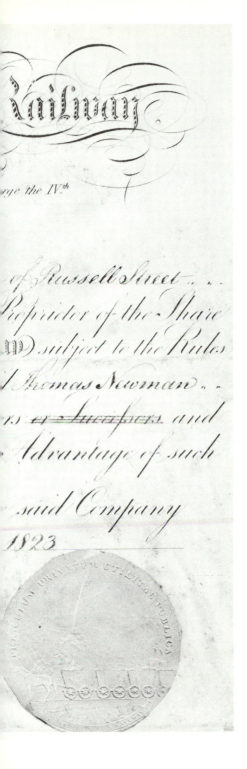

very impressed with George's knowledge and enthusiasm, and he at once arranged to visit Killingworth where he saw the line in operation. This convinced him that Stephenson was the man for his railway. When the Act of Parliament giving permission for the railway was finally passed in 1823, George was appointed chief engineer of the line. His salary was to be £300 a year. Work on the Stockton and Darlington Railway was started at once, and it was to be opened for traffic as soon as possible.

In October 1822, a year before this appointment, George had arranged for Robert, then aged nineteen, to take a short course at Edinburgh University. Here the young man went to the chemistry lectures of Dr. Hope, the natural philosophy lectures of Sir John Leslie, and the natural history class of Professor Jameson. He also went to evening classes in practical chemistry. All his notes from these lectures were taken home and fully discussed with his father. They were later bound and kept safe in his library. One of the subjects in which Robert took a special interest while at Edinburgh was geology, under Professor Jameson. This was to be of good use to him in his later life as a

A free ticket for the Stockton and Darlington, valid for five months.

construction engineer. These six months at university cost his father £80, but this was to be repaid over and over again in later years. It must be remembered that everything that Robert learned was passed on to and developed by his father.

Stephenson's first estimate of the cost of building the Stockton and Darlington Railway was £6,200. It did not mention the building of locomotives, although stationary engines were included, for he had seen at once that it would be impossible to use locomotives over the whole distance. To do so would have meant levelling the ground, and Mr. Pease was not prepared to pay for this. George Stephenson was always in favour of tunnels and embankments to help keep the track level. This is why so many of our

Digging cuttings was a long and difficult job. Here the railway workers are removing the earth from the cutting by means of wheelbarrows hauled up long platforms by pulleys.

railways today have cuttings and embankments. The original intention of the directors of the railway was to use horses, with fixed engines for the steep hills where horses would have been no good. After his visit to Killingworth, however, Edward Pease had become a convinced supporter of the locomotive, and he added a clause to his original Act allowing the use of steam engines to haul both goods and passengers.

Once appointed, Stephenson's first job was to survey the ground over which the line was to pass. He began work at once, with the help of his son Robert and a linesman. He would often call on Edward Pease and discuss the day's findings with him, and it was during one of these visits that Pease suggested that a factory should be bought in Newcastle for building locomotives. This idea was at once taken up by Stephenson, who still had the £1,000 from the safety-lamp, but he still had to borrow £500 each from Edward Pease and his friend Thomas Richardson. He bought a piece of land in Forth Street, Newcastle, in August 1823, and on this site a small building was erected. It became the centre of the great railway works which eventually developed. Locomotive building began early in 1824.

Although mainly interested in locomotives, Stephenson was also aware of the vital importance of a strong track. He tried interlocking the rails to give a smoother ride; the gauge was settled at 4 ft. 8½ in., the

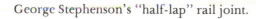

George Stephenson's "half-lap" rail joint.

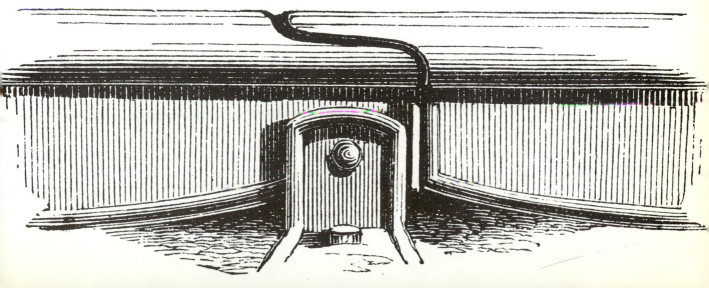

width of most of the local waggon axles. Thomas Meynell, the company chairman, laid the first of the new rails at Stockton on 23rd May, 1822.

While the railway was being constructed, engine building continued at full speed at the works of Robert Stephenson & Co. The first locomotive to be built there was the famous No. 1, later named *Locomotion*. It was a four-wheeled engine with its two cylinders mounted vertically in the boiler barrel. This, with the valve gear, displayed a mass of rods and wheels above the boiler. When in motion it must have

The engine *Locomotion* in 1825, the first to be built in the Stephensons' Forth Street works. This was the engine that pulled the train at the opening of the Stockton and Darlington Railway on 27th September, 1825.

Stephenson's 'Locomotion': Pride of the Stockton & Darlington Railway, 182

been very impressive. *Locomotion* may still be seen at Bank Top Station, Darlington, and there is a splendid model in the Science Museum at South Kensington, London.

Over three years were needed to build the railway. On 16th September, 1825, *Locomotion* left the Forth Street works. From there it was delivered by road to the Stockton and Darlington line, and the engine was put on the track at the Aycliffe Lane level crossing. After only eleven days "running in" it took part in the official opening of the line on 27th September, 1825.

Locomotion as it is today, on show at Bank Top Station, Darlington.

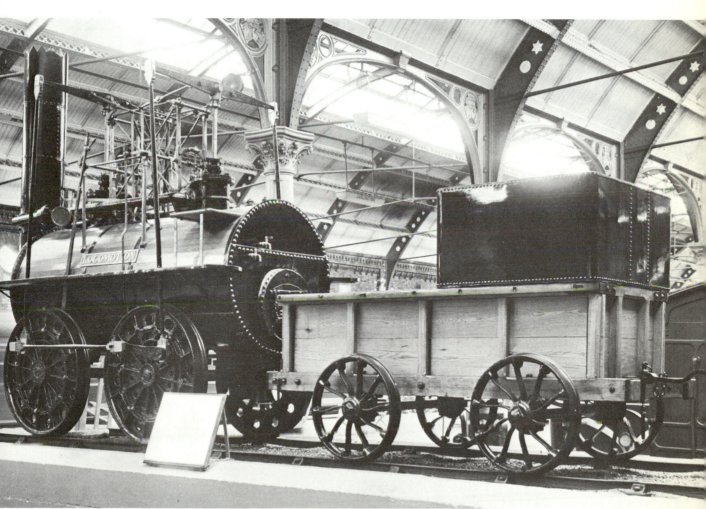

The day turned out fine and sunny and a great crowd covered the whole line. Stephenson's confidence in his engine cannot be better illustrated than by reproducing an extract from the hand-bill that he had published only two days after No. 1 was first put on the Stockton and Darlington track.

Above The scene at the opening of the Stockton and Darlington Railway.

Right The handbill announcing the opening of the line.

THE
STOCKTON & DARLINGTON
RAILWAY COMPANY
hereby give Notice,

THAT the FORMAL OPENING of their RAILWAY will take place on the 27th instant, as announced in the public Papers.—The Proprietors will assemble at the Permanent Steam Engine, situated below BRUSSELTON TOWER*, about nine Miles West of DARLINGTON at 8 o'clock, and after examining their extensive inclined Planes there, will start from the Foot of the BRUSSELTON descending Plane, at 9 o'clock, in the following Order :—

1. THE COMPANY'S LOCOMOTIVE ENGINE.
2. THE ENGINE'S TENDER, with Water and Coals.
3. SIX WAGGONS, laden with Coals, Merchandize, &c.
4. THE COMMITTEE, and other PROPRIETORS, in the COACH belonging to the COMPANY.
5. SIX WAGGONS, with Seats reserved for STRANGERS.
6. FOURTEEN WAGGONS, for the Conveyance of Workmen and others.

The WHOLE of the above to proceed to STOCKTON.

7. SIX WAGGONS, laden with Coals, to leave the Procession at the DARLINGTON BRANCH.
8. SIX WAGGONS, drawn by Horses, for Workmen and others.
9. Ditto   Ditto.
10. Ditto   Ditto.
11. Ditto   Ditto.

The COMPANY'S WORKMEN to leave the Procession at DARLINGTON, and DINE at that Place at ONE o'clock ; excepting those to whom Tickets are specially given for YARM, and for whom Conveyances will be provided, on their Arrival at STOCKTON.

TICKETS will be given to the Workmen who are to dine at DARLINGTON, specifying the Houses of Entertainment.

The PROPRIETORS, and such of the NOBILITY and GENTRY as may honour them with their Company, will DINE precisely at THREE o'clock, at the TOWN-HALL, STOCKTON.—Such of the Party as may incline to return to DARLINGTON that Evening, will find Conveyances in waiting for their Accommodation, to start from the COMPANY'S WHARF there precisely at SEVEN o'clock.

The COMPANY take this Opportunity of enjoining on all their WORK-PEOPLE that Attention to *Sobriety* and *Decorum* which they have hitherto had the Pleasure of observing.

The COMMITTEE give this PUBLIC NOTICE, that all Persons who shall ride upon, or by the sides of, the RAILWAY, on Horseback, will incur the Penalties imposed by the Acts of Parliament passed relative to this RAILWAY.

*Any Individuals desirous of seeing the TRAIN of Waggons descending the inclined Plane from ETHERLEY, and in Progress to BRUSSELTON, may have an Opportunity of so doing, by being on the RAILWAY at ST. HELEN'S AUCKLAND not later than Half-past Seven o'clock.

RAILWAY-OFFICE, *Sept. 19th*, 1825.

ATKINSON'S Office. High Row, Darlington.

His confidence was fully justified, for the whole of this ambitious programme went off without a hitch. *Locomotion*, which had been designed to pull only forty tons, successfully pulled over ninety tons from Brusselton to Stockton and often touched 12 miles per hour.

Locomotion continued in good working order until after 1846. In this year it was given pride of place at the opening of the Middlesbrough and Redcar Railway. It was fitting that this should be so, for the Stockton and Darlington Railway was directly concerned with the development of the town of Middlesbrough. In 1829 Edward Pease bought five hundred acres of land on the site of the future city, and extended the line from Stockton to the River Tees, so that coal could be loaded straight onto the waiting ships. Before the line was built, there was only a single farmhouse there, but soon docks were built and a busy town sprang up. In a few years Middlesbrough became one of the most thriving ports on the north-east coast of England.

5 The Liverpool and Manchester Railway

When the Stockton and Darlington Railway was completed, Robert Stephenson left England for South America. A group of businessmen in London, eager to make some money, had formed the Colombian Mining Association. They wanted to send some bright young engineer to Colombia, in South America, to dig silver and gold from the mines there; they would

Robert Stephenson as a young man.

then sell the precious metals, and keep the profits themselves.

When they offered the post to Robert, he was keen to accept. His father also thought he should go, for he was worried about his son's health, and thought that the warm climate would do him good. So the appointment was accepted, and Robert set sail.

He landed at La Guayra, in Venezuela, on 23rd July, 1824. His first job was to see if a railway could be built from there to Caracas, a few miles inland. Robert knew that earthquakes were frequent in that area, and decided that a railway would soon be broken up. He then started out by mule for Bogota, the capital of Colombia, and arrived there on 19th January, 1825. Then he travelled to Mariquita, where he made his headquarters, and waited for the party of Cornish miners who were to work for him to arrive from England.

When the Cornishmen arrived, they caused a great deal of trouble. They drank all the time, and behaved so badly in the town that Robert had to move the whole group up into the mountains, away from the furious people of Mariquita. At last they reached Santa Ana, where they were to start digging for gold and silver.

After the scorching heat of the plains, the coolness and the tropical plants of the mountains must have made Santa Ana seem like paradise. But Robert's troubles were by no means over, for the men who were meant to be working for him did their best to make life as difficult as possible, and it was only with great patience and strength of character that he overcame this problem.

Despite Robert's skill, the mining was not a success. The businessmen of the Colombian Mining Association had not even bothered to find out if the project was possible, and it was not. The mining methods that had been so successful in Cornwall and Northumberland were not suited to the mountains of

50

Robert Stephenson's cottage at Santa Ana, where he lived during his mining operations in South America.

South America. Robert was very disappointed. By 1826, knowing how much his father needed him at home, he made up his mind not to renew his three year contract. As things turned out, he was quite right to come home.

He still had more adventures to come, however, for during the voyage home he was ship-wrecked. He had decided to sail via New York, and when the ship was within one day's sailing from there it was caught in a hurricane and driven onto the rocks. Robert managed to get safely ashore before the ship broke up completely, but all his baggage and money were lost. This

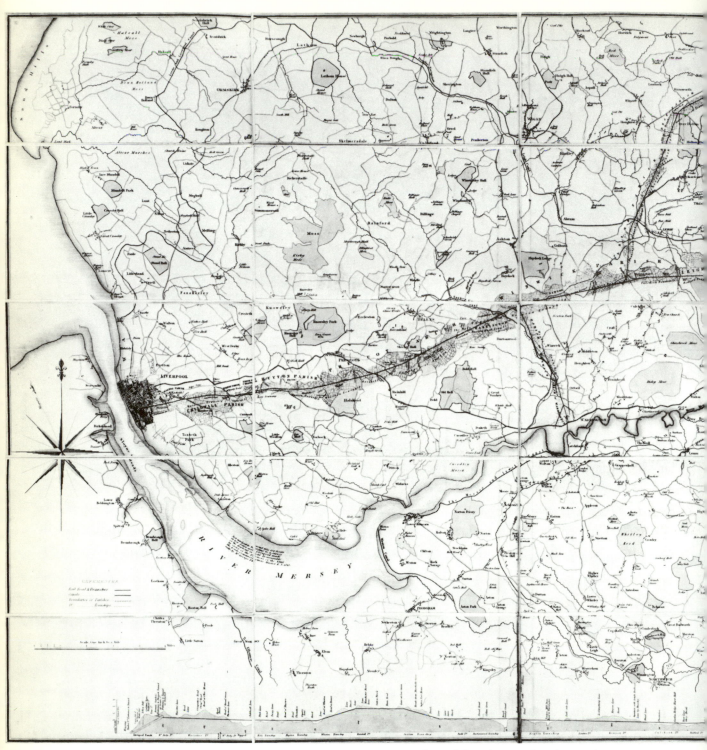

A plan of the Liverpool and Manchester
Railway in 1829. This was to be the first
passenger carrying line in the world.

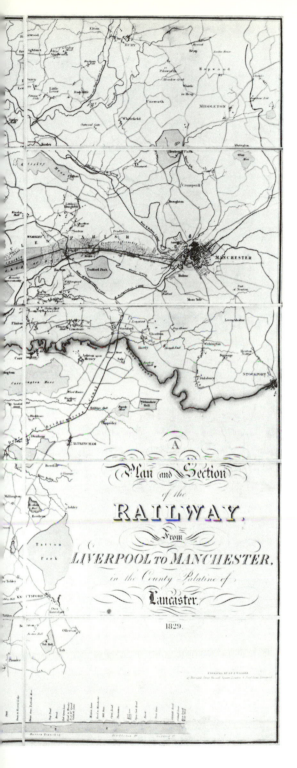

was how he first arrived in the United States! He made the best of the accident, and went on a sight-seeing tour of North America before finally sailing for home.

Meanwhile, in England, George Stephenson had been offered the post of chief engineer to a railway which was to become the first passenger carrying line in the world—the Liverpool and Manchester Railway. The bill to allow the line to be built was debated in the House of Commons on 21st March, 1825. Many people were very much against railways at this time. Country landowners objected strongly, as did many country lovers. Farmers feared for the health of their cattle. Householders were told that sparks from the engine's chimney would set fire to their property. Perhaps it was because of all these objections that the Liverpool and Manchester bill failed, by a single vote, to become law.

After this setback, it seemed that all George Stephenson's planning was worthless. His dream of a great railway between the two thriving northern cities was at an end. Nevertheless, the Company decided to make another attempt to get the bill passed. A new survey was made in 1826 by two nationally known engineers named George and John Rennie (1791 – 1866, and 1794 – 1874). This time there was less opposition, and permission to build the railway was given. The Company immediately confirmed their faith in George Stephenson by appointing him chief engineer at a salary of £1,000 a year. He promptly accepted their offer and at once set about the task with all his usual enthusiasm.

He showed his determination by beginning to lay the line across Chat Moss. This was a seemingly bottomless bog at the Manchester end of the project. At first he laid a footpath of heather along the proposed route. This, at least, supported a man without sinking. Then he laid a single track of railway, along which he ran the building material waggons. Each truck carried about a ton. Meanwhile drains were dug on each side,

Olive Mount cutting, on the Liverpool and Manchester line. The sandstone rock was blasted out, and huge blocks of it were used to build the Sankey viaduct. The cutting was nearly two miles long.

but they quickly filled in. After weeks of work, little visible progress could be seen. Rumours spread about the area that many of the workmen had been drowned in Chat Moss. The directors became worried about the cost of the operation, but Stephenson didn't lose heart. Eventually, success crowned his efforts.

At the western end of the line a very deep sandstone cutting had to be made at Olive Mount, and the tunnel under Liverpool proved very difficult to build. Sixty-three bridges or viaducts had to be built along the line, and there were some remarkable engineering feats among these works. At last the first experimental train made the crossing of Chat Moss. As it turned out, the line across the Moss cost only one tenth of the sum set aside for it.

During this period Stephenson gathered together the first of what were to become the railway navvies. These were men who worked on the railways all over Britain, and their achievements were enormous. They wandered from one project to the next, living in rough wooden huts which they took down and moved when their work was done. Most of them were unable to read. Yet they came to have a high degree of knowledge about the properties of clay and rock, and their skill in the art of tunnelling was considerable. Often they worked sixteen hours a day. They were careless of danger; the result was that accidents were all too frequent.

Now Robert was on his way home, and he reached England aboard the S.S. *Pacific* in November 1827. Father and son were reunited when Robert stepped ashore. They were both changed. George saw before him a sunburnt, confident young man of the world. He had lost his Northumbrian accent and spoke with a polished voice. Robert noticed that his father, who was now forty-six years old, looked fit and well, although his hair had turned quite white. All in all the adventure in South America had given young Stephenson great confidence, in spite of the rather poor financial return. After meeting his father he set out from Liverpool for Newcastle and his Forth Street locomotive works.

There he found his factory to be in a very poor state. It had run down during his absence abroad, for his father had been too busy with the Liverpool and Manchester Railway to spare it much time. He started to put affairs in order but there was much to do. It was at about this time that the directors of the Liverpool and Manchester Railway were discussing one vital problem which had still to be settled. Were they to use horses or steam engines to pull the waggons? George himself was never in any doubt. He wanted steam locomotives. He kept pointing out to his directors that his engines were better in every respect than horses. Eventually they were persuaded that the steam engine should at least be given a fair trial. Then someone had a brilliant idea. It was decided to hold a competition with a prize of £500 offered to the builder of the most efficient engine. Locomotive engineers throughout the country knew how important the winning of this prize would be to their companies. There were many short railway lines all over England and Wales; the directors of these lines would study the results of the competition, and they would order engines from the successful entrant.

George and Robert Stephenson were determined to win the competition. The locomotive they would enter was going to be the best the Forth Street works could produce.

6 *The Rocket*

Robert was now in charge of locomotive building at
the workshop in Newcastle. During experiments
made before the competition was announced he had
discovered a solution to the high pressure steam
problems which were worrying all locomotive
engineers. The difficulty was to produce as much high
pressure steam as possible. To do this, Robert inserted twenty-five copper tubes of three inches
diameter into the boilers. These were filled with hot
water from the boiler. This greatly increased the
power of the engine because the tubes provided a
greater heating surface for the hot gases passing to the
funnel. When the engine was finally completed it was
tested on the Killingworth line. As soon as Robert was
satisfied with its performance he wrote and told his
father that it would be ready for the trial, which was to
be held at Rainhill on 1st October, 1829. Robert's
engine was christened the *Rocket*.

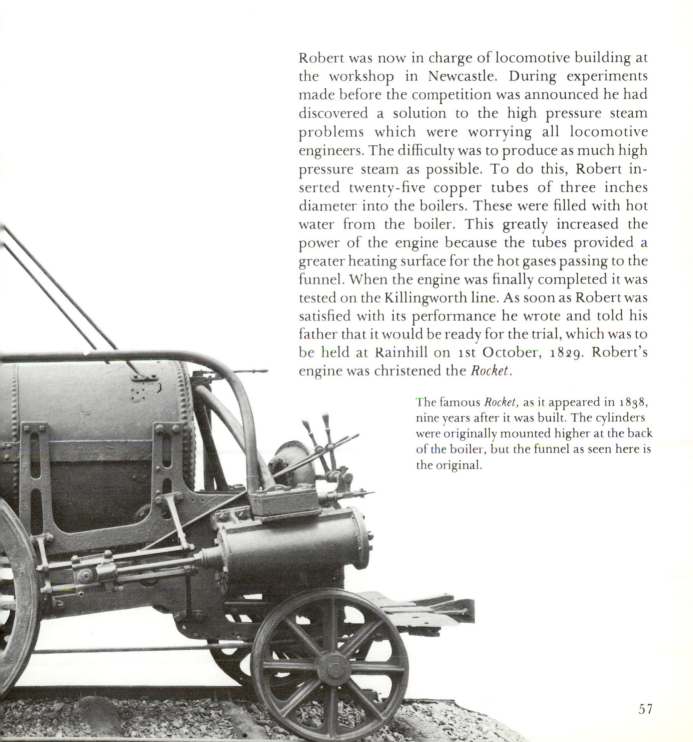

The famous *Rocket,* as it appeared in 1838,
nine years after it was built. The cylinders
were originally mounted higher at the back
of the boiler, but the funnel as seen here is
the original.

The competition had seized the imagination of the public and a great crowd gathered at Rainhill on 6th October. The date had been put back five days to allow the engineers extra time to get their engines into "racing" trim. There were four entrants, as follows:

No. 1 Messrs Braithwaite and Ericsson's *Novelty*
No. 2 Mr. Timothy Hackworth's *Sanspareil*
No. 3 Messrs Stephenson & Co.'s *Rocket*
No. 4 Mr. Burstall's *Perseverance*

Others which had been entered could not be got ready in time.

A special stand had been built, with flags flying, and literally thousands of people were there to get a good view. The stretch of track over which the engines were to be tried was level, and about two miles long. Each engine was to be tested separately and on different days. During the day the engine was to complete twenty trips, totalling about eighty miles. The

The scene at the Rainhill trials on 6th October, 1829. The artist has drawn the *Rocket* at the head of the procession, Timothy Hackworth's *Sanspareil* second, and the *Novelty* of Braithwaite and Ericsson last.

minimum speed required was ten miles per hour.

Novelty was the favourite, mainly because of her pleasant lines and general neatness. But the *Rocket* was the first to be ready, and was ordered out straight away. She successfully ran six trips (twelve miles) in fifty-three minutes. *Novelty* was next asked to show her paces and she ran almost twice as fast as the Newcastle engine. It then started to rain, and the down-pour caused the postponement of the proceedings until the next day. It was then found that *Sanspareil* needed boiler repairs and *Novelty* had collapsed bellows. To keep the crowd of people interested, George again brought out the willing *Rocket*. A coach was loaded with thirty brave spectators and amidst great excitement they were given a run along the track. They travelled at more than twenty miles per hour.

Perseverance had already withdrawn when it was found that she could not exceed five miles per hour. So *Rocket* was the only engine that had so far fulfilled all the conditions of the competition. The final test took place six days later when, much to the dismay of her supporters, *Novelty* broke down yet again, and Stephenson's engine became the outright winner of the contest. He was duly awarded the £500 prize.

Nothing further was heard of horse transport for the Liverpool and Manchester Railway. The thirty-four mile line was completed in less than four years. George Stephenson and his assistant engineers had done a superb job. Some six hundred navvies had been employed; later, at the height of the railway boom, a quarter of a million were engaged in building railways. By 1851 over six thousand miles of track had been laid in the United Kingdom.

The official opening of the Liverpool and Manchester Railway in September 1830 was a historic occasion, but it was marred by a fatal accident to a distinguished politician. The victim was William Huskisson (1770 – 1830), the leader of what would now be called the "left wing" of the Conservative par-

The opening of the Liverpool and
Manchester Railway. This engraving shows
the Moorish arch at Edge Hill as it appeared
on the day.

ty. On the great day eight special trains set out from
Crown Street Station, Liverpool. The most important
of the one thousand travellers were the Duke of
Wellington and the ill-fated Mr. Huskisson. Their
parliamentary party rode in a splendid coach with a
crimson canopy supported by golden pillars. The
canopy had to be lowered when they came to bridges.

The accident happened when the train carrying this
party stopped to let the passengers watch the other
trains, which were running on a track very close by.
Huskisson had got out of the coach and was talking to
the Duke, when the *Rocket* came speeding along the
other line. In the confusion Huskisson stumbled and
fell beneath the engine's wheels. His leg was horribly

A replica of the *Northumbrian* locomotive, which was built at the Forth Street locomotive works by George and Robert Stephenson. Although the engine resembles the *Rocket,* it has the appearance of some of the more modern steam locomotives of this century.

crushed, and he died that same evening.

Despite this unlucky incident at the opening, the railway proved to be a great success. Steam power was finally accepted for the splendid thing it undoubtedly was. The line was shown to be a potential gold mine and the number of passengers multiplied rapidly. It was now possible for merchants to conduct their business in Liverpool or Manchester and return to their own city on the same day.

Work in the Forth Street factory was now going at full speed and seven more locomotives were built there for the Liverpool and Manchester Railway. These were named *Meteor, Comet, Dart, Arrow, Phoenix, North Star* and *Northumbrian.* At the time of the

1888·265

LEICESTER & SWANNINGTON RAILWAY COMPANY.

OLD BRASS RAILWAY PASSENGER TICKET
IN USE FROM THE OPENING OF THE ABOVE RAILWAY
ON JULY 17TH, 1832, TO THE YEAR 1846 WHEN THE ABOVE
LINE BECAME THE PROPERTY OF THE MIDLAND COMPANY

PRESENTED BY CLEMENT E. STRETTON, ESQ. C.E.

L & S
RAILWAY
BAGWORTH
No 20

A PASSENGER GOING TO BAGWORTH FROM ANY OTHER STATION
WOULD HAVE A NUMBERED TICKET ISSUED TO HIM (No 20 IN
THIS INSTANCE), AND THE NUMBER OF TICKET, AND FARE
PAID, RECORDED IN A BOOK.
THE GUARD OF THE TRAIN CARRIED A COLLECTING
BOX HAVING A SEPARATE DIVISION FOR
EACH STATION, AND AFTER THE COLLECTION
OF TICKETS, THEY WERE RETURNED TO
THE VARIOUS STATIONS, TO BE
AGAIN USED.

There have been many forms of ticket since the railways began. This one, for the Leicester and Swannington Railway, is made of metal, and had to be handed in at the end of the journey, to be re-used.

opening of the railway the *Northumbrian* was reckoned to be the most up to date engine on the line. But Robert Stephenson was making such rapid improvements in design that a locomotive was delivered to Liverpool in October 1830 which outclassed all the company's other engines. This was the famous *Planet*. She was followed a year later by the *Samson* and her sister engine, the *Goliath*. Robert built these engines specially for the steep hills, and they could haul ninety tons up the inclines and 200 tons on the level.

The superiority of Stephenson's engines was firmly established, and they were often copied by other engine builders. The Newcastle workshops became a training school for engineers and drivers. Such trained men were required not only in Britain, but all over Europe, for the building of new railways.

While the Liverpool and Manchester line was being built, George Stephenson was consulted about a short line to be built near Leicester. This was called the Leicester and Swannington Railway. The line was needed to link up the coalfields of west Leicestershire with the town of Leicester. There were difficulties over paying for the line, but after making his survey George offered to raise the money and his proposal was accepted. He was invited to become engineer of the line, but he declined, in view of all the other work he had in hand. Instead he recommended his son for the job. Robert was then twenty-seven years of age. He got on with the construction of the sixteen mile line, which was completed to everyone's satisfaction.

While engaged in this work he noticed an advertisement for the sale of a piece of local land. With his knowledge of the land he became convinced that there was coal underground. He advised his father to buy the property, which was at Snibston, near Ashby de la Zouch, in Leicestershire. The estate was bought by George Stephenson, and a pit was sunk there. Robert was right about the coal, and eventually George was able to send the first train of coal from his property to Leicester. He proved to be a very good colliery owner and his workmen were always well looked after. They were given a school and a church of their own.

George Stephenson had moved house from Liverpool to Alton Grange, near Leicester, when the pit was bought. With everything running well in Leicestershire the Stephensons were now ready for their next job. This turned out to be the most important railway project in which they were ever involved—the London and Birmingham Railway.

George Stephenson's home at Alton Grange, in Leicestershire.

7 The London and Birmingham Railway

When the London and Birmingham Railway was proposed in 1830, the promoters asked George Stephenson to advise them over the route it was to take. This he did, with all his usual care, and he was offered the post of joint engineer with Francis Giles (1787 – 1847). George thought that this man was incompetent, and he refused to share the responsibility with him. Then the directors decided to offer the post to George and his son. After discussing the matter in a churchyard near to the directors' meeting place, they decided to accept the offer. Robert Stephenson was appointed engineer in chief with a salary of £1,500 a year.

He had been married in 1829 to Fanny Sanderson, the daughter of a City merchant, and the couple now moved their home from Newcastle to London. Here they took a house on Haverstock Hill, and they lived there throughout the construction of the London and Birmingham Railway.

The building of this line came about because of the great growth of industry in Birmingham and the Black Country of the Midlands, where the scope for more trade was being held up by the lack of fast and efficient transport. For instance, to send small parcels of made up goods by stage-coach took three days, and more bulky goods sent by canal took much longer. Delays and stealing added to the difficulties. During the winter, frost often caused complete shut down. In the early 1830's one thousand tons of goods were sent every week from Birmingham to London by canal. Orders were often lost because of late delivery, especially goods being sent abroad. Because of all this, trade was being held up.

It might be thought, then, that everyone would

have been pleased to welcome the railways. But this was not so. Many people were bitterly opposed to the new line. The landowners of Northampton forced the builders to make the line pass some distance from their town, and the company had to agree to develop their locomotive works at Wolverton instead of at Northampton, so that they would not interfere with the private land around the town. The results of having to change their plans were expensive.

In order to pass five miles from Northampton they had to build the Kilsby tunnel. This was a very difficult operation, and cost £300,000. There were seven other

Work in progress in the Kilsby tunnel. One of the ventilating shafts mentioned on the next page is being used to remove rubble from the digging.

Navvies at work digging a cutting. It was thanks to these dedicated and hard-working men that so much progress was made in the building of the railways during the nineteenth century.

tunnels to be built between London and Birmingham. The Kilsby tunnel is 2,400 yards long, and it was the longest tunnel to be built at that time. Many thought that passengers would suffocate in the dark. Because of this Robert Stephenson built two large ventilating shafts to allow the smoke and steam of the engines to escape.

A thousand workmen lived in Kilsby during the building of the tunnel, and there were many fights and brawls between the navvies and the villagers. The construction of this railway was compared by Samuel Smiles (1812 – 1904), the Victorian biographer of

George Stephenson, with the greatest engineering feat then known—the building of the Pyramids in Egypt. The work on the Pyramids took thirty thousand men over twenty years to complete. The London and Birmingham Railway took twenty thousand men less than five years. It was built in spite of many obstructions, and without the harsh methods used by the Egyptian King who supervised the building of the Pyramids.

The total cost of building the railway was £5,500,000. This works out at £50,000 for every mile. The Kilsby tunnel was the last stretch of line to be completed. On 21st June, 1838, George and Robert Stephenson were both present at Kilsby when the last brick was laid, with a silver trowel. The following Sunday, June 24th, a 9.30 a.m. train from Euston ran through to Curzon Street, the Birmingham station, and at 10.00 a.m. an up train left Birmingham for London.

The line was officially opened on 17th September, 1838. George Stephenson was on the footplate of the special train which brought the directors to Birmingham.

Soon after this a huge gateway designed by Philip Hardwick (1792 – 1870) was erected outside Euston Station. This was the gateway to the first great main line railway. It had to be demolished in 1963.

George and Robert Stephenson were by now much in demand as railway builders. In the three years 1835 to 1837 they had travelled twenty thousand miles, mostly by stage coach. After the completion of the London and Birmingham line they were responsible for many superb feats of engineering. Before describing the iron tubular bridges for which Robert is justly famous, George's many viaducts should be remembered.

Among these was the famous Dutton viaduct, built in 1836 on the Grand Junction Railway which runs from Warrington to Birmingham. This has twenty

The Doric Portico built for the entrance to Euston Station after the opening of the London and Birmingham Railway.

LONDON AND BIRMINGHAM RAILWAY.

ENTRANCE FRONT OF THE LONDON STATION.

George Stephenson in later life. This portrait shows him standing in front of a scene from the Liverpool and Manchester Railway, at Chat Moss. The building of this stretch of line was considered to be one of his greatest achievements.

arches, each spanning sixty feet. The piers were built on piles which were sunk twenty feet deep. It is considered by many to be the finest of all George Stephenson's viaducts.

The London and Birmingham Railway was always his favourite line, but he also had a soft spot for the new Midland Railway. This ran through a rich mining district and gave access to many coal-fields. When he was asked to become chief engineer of the North Midland over the $72\frac{1}{2}$ miles between Derby and Leeds, he accepted at once.

This superbly engineered line has two hundred bridges and seven tunnels. It took him three years to build and cost three million pounds. George Stephenson was sure that it would become a profitable line. He arranged for it to be extended to York, and became a shareholder in the company. After he retired he bought a house by the side of the line, and used to "watch the trains go by."

In his early days at Killingworth he had forecast that the post from London to Newcastle would be brought by steam train. When the North Midland Railway was opened on 11th March, 1840, the mail train from London was able to get as far as York. He sometimes wondered if he would live to see his prediction come true, for he was now fifty-nine years old.

At this time he was engaged on other railways all over the country. Among these was the Newcastle to Edinburgh line. This was meant to complete the main line north from London.

There was one instance where his advice was not accepted. This concerned the line from Preston to Carlisle. George Stephenson recommended a route via Whitehaven and Maryport, skirting the mountains of the Lake District. It was a long way round. Because of this the directors accepted the plan of Joseph Locke (1805 – 1860). His route went straight through the mountains and over Shap Fell. This very severe gradient is a test of even the most modern locomotives. It must have been a fearsome task for the little engines of those days.

George continued to live at Alton Grange, but he was so busy that he was often away for months at a time. He had so much work to do that he had to employ a secretary, and he took this man with him on all his journeys. His own writing was still not very good, no doubt because of the poor start he had in life, but he was a very good dictator of letters.

In spite of the busy life he led he kept up his boyhood interest in wild birds. He also loved to spend his spare time in the garden. The amount of business he had to deal with grew so much that he and Robert opened a London office, first at 9 Duke Street, Westminster, and later at $30\frac{1}{2}$ George Street. Many important meetings took place there. At about this time he visited Belgium to advise the railway engineers there over their national railway system.

The Stephensons finished many lines after the completion of the London and Birmingham Railway. By 1840, in fact, they had built over three hundred miles of railway at a cost of eleven million pounds.

8 George's Retirement

The career of George Stephenson was now beginning to draw to a close. On his return from a visit to Spain in September 1845 he had an attack of pleurisy. This was a danger signal which even he could not ignore. As it turned out he had only three more years to live. He now began a partial retirement.

In 1843 he had leased Tapton House at Stony Middleton in Derbyshire, overlooking his much loved Midland Railway, and he now moved there from Alton Grange. The gardens there were the great in-

Tapton House, at Chesterfield, George Stephenson's retirement home.

terest of his old age. He built some large greenhouses and his fruit took many prizes; often he would give apricots, grapes and peaches to his employees. When he was working at Killingworth he used to get great pleasure from growing larger cabbages and cauliflowers than his neighbours. Now, with his great wealth, he was able to follow his hobby on a much greater scale. His greatest rival in this was the Duke of Devonshire who lived at Chatsworth, nearby.

He took little part in the exciting events taking place at this time in the railway world, but he was still very interested in his son's progress and achievements.

During his father's retirement Robert was involved as engineer in no fewer than thirty-three new

Robert Stephenson's railway viaduct over the Tweed, at Berwick.

schemes. One of these was the line between Newcastle and Berwick. He built at Berwick a magnificent viaduct with twenty-eight arches, 126 ft. above the river bed. It is still there to this day, and you can stand in the ruined Berwick Castle and watch the modern Flying Scotsman thunder across. It was opened by Queen Victoria on the 28th August, 1850.

On the same line Robert constructed the High Level bridge across the Tyne, between Newcastle and Gateshead. The river here is 500 ft. wide and the bridge had to be over 1,000 ft. long. It is in the form of a bow-and-string girder. All the ironwork for the bridge was made at Newcastle. The two great bridges over the Tyne and the Tweed completed the East Coast route to Scotland.

The bow-and-string construction of the High Level bridge at Newcastle is clearly shown in this plan. The bridge, still in use today, carries trains on the upper level, and cars on the lower, with a footpath on either side.

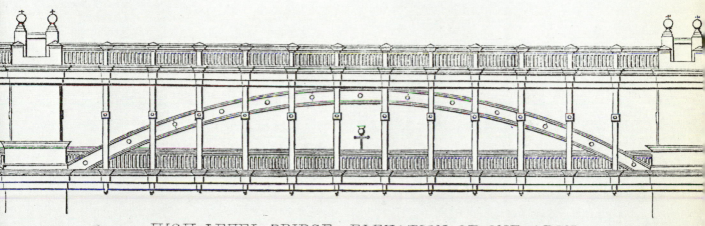

HIGH LEVEL BRIDGE—ELEVATION OF ONE ARCH.

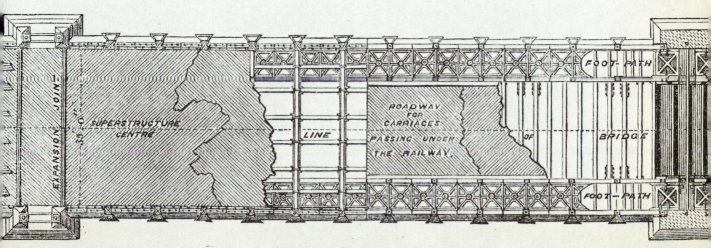

PLAN OF ONE ARCH.

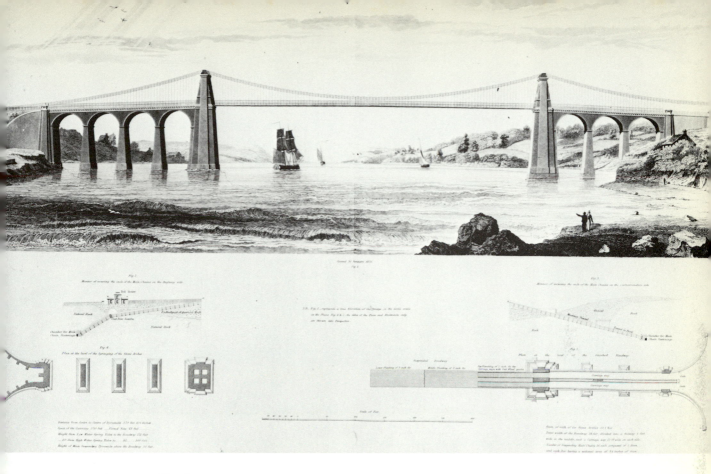

Above   Thomas Telford's suspension bridge over the Menai Straits, with details of its construction below. Telford was the foremost civil engineer of his time, and he built many fine bridges and viaducts. His Menai bridge was opened in 1825.

While all this work was being done on the East Coast route, The Chester and Holyhead line was being built. Another great bridge was planned to cross the Menai Straits. This was begun by George and completed by Robert. There was already a suspension bridge across the Straits, built by Thomas Telford (1757 – 1834) twenty years before. It was decided that the best way of building the almost quarter mile long bridge was by means of huge box girders, which had to be one hundred feet above the water. Sir William Fairbairn, mentioned in chapter one, helped the Stephensons by making a large model of the proposed bridge at his works in Millwall. This model was seventy-five feet long, and it was tested until it gave way.

The final design of the bridge was based on these experiments. Luckily there was a rock in the middle of

Left   A view of Newcastle showing the High Level bridge as it was when newly built.

the Menai Straits. It was called the Britannia rock and became the central pier of the structures. The wrought iron tubes were built in sections on the shore, on floating pontoons. When they were ready, they were hauled out into position against the masonry piers. The job was done at high tide, and as the tide fell the pontoons floated away, leaving the box sections remaining supported at the ends. Powerful hydraulic apparatus was used as the masonry was built up; the tubes were raised over and over again until they reached the desired height. The bridge was completed on 5th March, 1850. The first train to cross carried

The Britannia bridge during the early stages of its construction. The Britannia rock, foundation of the central pier of the bridge, can be clearly seen.

The completed bridge.

one thousand passengers and was hauled by three locomotives. It passed over safely. The bridge was opened for regular traffic on 18th March, 1850. It became known as the Britannia bridge. The foundation stone had been laid on 10th April, 1846; the bridge had taken four years to build.

The Britannia bridge is still in use and is strong enough to support the heaviest engines of modern times. It was damaged by fire recently, but has now been repaired, and is in regular use again, 125 years after it was built.

The success of this bridge caused Robert Stephen-

Left A sketch of Robert Stephenson, taken for the *Illustrated London News,* when he became Member of Parliament for Whitby. He was then aged forty-four.

Right A railway map of Egypt, showing the line built by Robert Stephenson from Alexandria to Cairo. Robert travelled widely during his later years, and contributed to the development of the railways wherever he went.

son to design other tubular bridges. These will be discussed in the next chapter. The mighty bridge and the completion of the Chester and Holyhead line led to the formation of England's foremost railway company. This was the London and North Western Railway Company. Its main lines were from London to Holyhead and from London to Carlisle.

In 1847 Robert became the Member of Parliament for Whitby, in his native Northumberland. At about this time he built the Egyptian State Railway between Cairo and Alexandria.

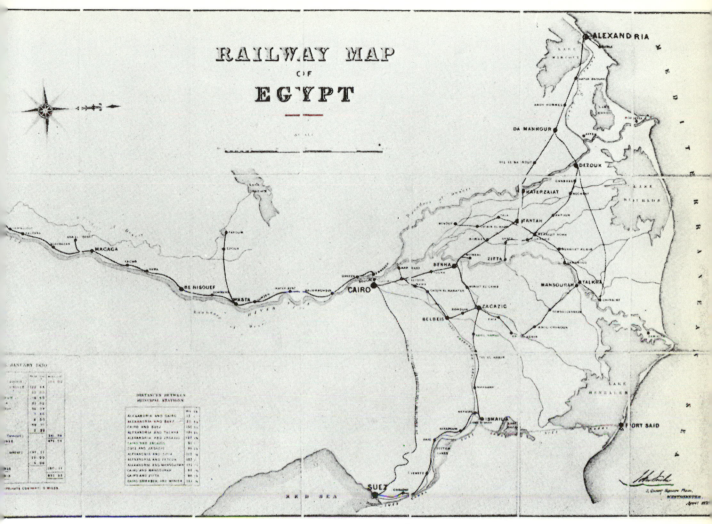

George Stephenson was now fully retired. He enjoyed inviting the humble friends of his early days to his house; he had never become snobbish or over-bearing. Occasionally he went up to London, and he enjoyed making visits to the North East. In 1847, the year before he died, he was present at the opening of the Trent Valley Railway. This was one of the lines which he had originally surveyed, many years before. After this there were few outings, and he spent his days quietly with his animals and his birds and his gardening.

The statue of George Stephenson erected in the Great Hall, at Euston Station. Euston was the London terminus of the London and Birmingham Railway when it was opened in 1838.

In 1845, to his great sorrow, his faithful wife Elizabeth had died. In 1848 he married again. He took as his third wife his housekeeper, Miss Gregory, the daughter of a farmer near Bakewell. His health was now very delicate, but he remained quite active, and he was well enough to go to the meeting of the Mechanical Institute in Birmingham on the 27th July, 1848. Shortly after this he had a second attack of pleurisy, and although carefully nursed by his wife day and night, he died on 12th August, 1848. He was in his sixty-seventh year. No longer were the engine-men to see his familiar figure, which had so often stood on the slopes of Tapton hill as he watched the expresses roar past.

He was buried in Trinity Church at Chesterfield on 16th August, 1848. Among those who attended the ceremony was Edward Pease, who was then eighty years old. A statue of George Stephenson, commissioned by the directors of the London and North Western Railway, was placed in St. George's Hall, Liverpool. A few years later another was erected in the Great Hall at Euston Station. There is also a particularly fine statue of him at Newcastle, close to his locomotive works and near to Robert's High Level bridge.

9 *Robert's Last Achievements*

After his father's death Robert continued to extend his locomotive factory at Newcastle. He also undertook many engineering jobs. Among these he designed two bridges in Egypt, one over the Nile, at Benha, the other over the Karrineen Canal, at Birket-el-Saba. They were similar to the Britannia bridge in Wales, and were both opened in October 1855.

Later Robert was the designer of the magnificent Victoria bridge at Montreal in Canada. This was five times longer than the bridge across the Menai Straits; it extended almost two miles across the St. Lawrence River. All the ironwork for this bridge was made in

Below Edward VII, Prince of Wales, closing the last rivet of Robert Stephenson's Victoria bridge over the St. Lawrence river in Canada. A sketch made on the spot, from the *Illustrated London News* of 6th October, 1860.

Above The opening of the Victoria bridge by the Prince of Wales.

England at the Canada Works at Birkenhead. It was shipped across the Atlantic, prepared and ready for fixing. More than eight thousand tons of iron were delivered in this way.

The bridge engineers were lucky in that the St. Lawrence at Montreal is quite shallow. This helped greatly with the pier foundations. Despite this advantage, they had the weather against them; for half the year the river was iced over. It was the greatest of all Robert's bridges. Unfortunately he did not live to see it completed. Work began in April, 1854, but the first train did not cross until 24th November, 1859. The official opening by Edward VII, Prince of Wales, was on 25th August, 1860.

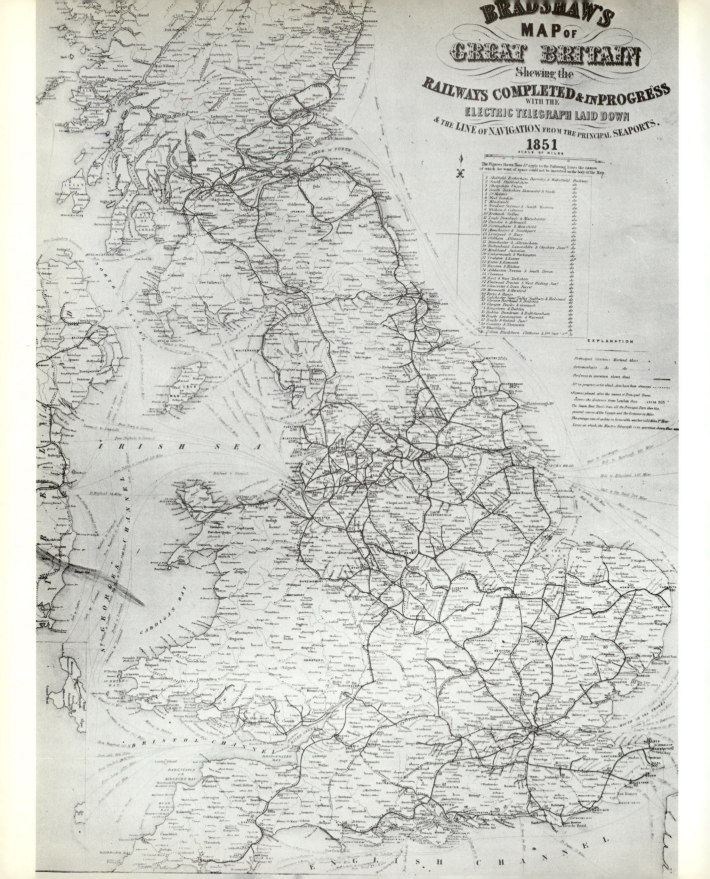

BRADSHAW'S MAP OF GREAT BRITAIN

Shewing the

RAILWAYS COMPLETED & IN PROGRESS

WITH THE

ELECTRIC TELEGRAPH LAID DOWN

& THE LINE OF NAVIGATION FROM THE PRINCIPAL SEAPORTS.

1851

SCALE OF MILES

The Figures Shewn thus 12 apply to the Following Lines the names
of which for want of space could not be inserted on the body of the Map.

1 Ashfield Rotherham Barnsley & Wakefield Railway
2 South Staffordshire   do
3 Shropshire Union   do
4 South Yorkshire Doncaster & Goole   do
5 St Helens   do
6 West London   do
7 Blackwall   do
8 Windsor Staines & South Western   do
9 Wilts & Calleuns   do
10 Erewash Valley   do
11 Leeds Dewsbury & Manchester   do
12 Dundee & Arbroath   do
13 Nottingham & Mansfield   do
14 Manchester & Southport   do
15 Liverpool & Bury   do
16 Oldham Alliance   do
17 Manchester & Altrincham   do
18 Birkenhead Lancashire & Cheshire Junc   do
19 Monkland Junction   do
20 Cockermouth & Workington do
21 Trent Valley & Luine   do
22 Leven & Lismouth   do
23 Buxton & Bixton   do
24 Libberton Newton & South Devon   do
25 Florence   do
26 East & West Yorkshire   do
27 Fleetwood Preston & West Riding Junc   do
28 Gloucester & Dean Forest do
29 Monmouth & Hereford   do
30 Berks & Hants   do
31 Colchester Stour Valley Sudbury & Halstead   do
32 Eastern Counties & Brighton   do
33 Glasgow Paisley & Greenock   do
34 Kingstown & Dublin   do
35 Dublin Drogheda & Rathfarnham   do
36 Royal Leamington & Warwick do
37 Rugby & Oxford Junc   do
38 Coventry & Nuneaton   do
39 Blackfield   do
40 Fulton Blackburn Clitheroe & N.E Junc   do

EXPLANATION

Principal Stations Marked thus
Intermediate   do   do
Railways in operation, shown thus
Do. in progress or for which Acts have been obtained
Figures placed after the names of Principal Towns   LEEDS 205
Dynes the distance from London thus
The Steam Boat Track from all the Principal Ports thus the
graduated course of the Voyage and the distance in Miles.
The average rate of sailing in Seven miles another is ½ Hour
Lines on which the Electric Telegraph is in operation shown thus

By 1851, three years after George Stephenson's death, most of Britain was connected by railways; many of these were built by George and Robert Stephenson.

By the 1940's the massive stone work of the piers had at last begun to show signs of wear. This is not surprising when it is remembered that it had been surrounded by pack-ice every winter for eighty years. Thanks to modern repair methods it has been completely restored, and it could well last for yet another eighty years. The whole structure is a fine memorial to Robert Stephenson, and to all British engineers.

In 1850 Robert was only forty-seven years of age, but the last ten busy years had aged him greatly. He was never again really fit. He was, of course, very wealthy, with an annual income of £30,000, a very high figure in those days. He received many awards from the foreign governments that he had served. These included the French Legion of Honour, which was presented to him at the Paris Exhibition of 1855, but he had refused a knighthood, as had his father before him. He did accept his election to be a Fellow of The Royal Society.*

Now he had no wife or children to live for, and at heart he was a sad and lonely man. He spent a lot of time at his clubs, and seemed reluctant to return to the loneliness of his large London house at 34, Gloucester Square. Such was his life during his last years. He was always thinking back to the time he had spent with his beloved wife at Newcastle.

Yet his last years were not all dreary. He had a yacht of his own, which was built for him by John Scott Russell (1808 – 1882). It was a vessel of 100 tons, and was named *Titania*. Russell was a famous ship-builder who also built the *Great Eastern*. His first long voyage in her was to Alexandria, from where he had built the railway to Cairo. Robert found that the dry desert air was good for his health. He had many friends whom he took sailing; among these was his one-time rival Isambard Kingdom Brunel (1806 – 1859). They became very close friends as death drew nearer to them both. Brunel had been present when the Britannia bridge tubes were floated, and was a valuable

*A society concerned with new developments in all branches of science.

MEMENTO MORI.

DUST TO DUST.

BRITANNIA BRIDGE.

S

HIGH LEVEL BRIDGE.

VICTORIA BRIDGE.

A page from the *Illustrated London News* of 19th October, 1859, showing Robert Stephenson's funeral in Westminster Abbey, and some of his famous bridges.

companion to Robert at the end of his life.

Robert Stephenson never really retired like his father. Of course, he was now able to work only when he chose, but he still kept up his engineering skill. He now built the railway from Christiana to Lake Miosen in Norway. For this work the King of Norway awarded him the Order of St. Olaf.

It was after a voyage in *Titania* to Norway in 1859 that his last illness seized him. He died on 12th October, 1859, aged fifty-six years. He was buried in Westminster Abbey alongside Thomas Telford, the great road and canal engineer. This was an honour which he well deserved, for he too was one of England's greatest engineers.

The lives of George and Robert Stephenson speak for themselves. They were born in a state of the direst poverty, yet their richness of spirit enabled them to rise above it. To such a degree did they rise that Robert eventually became a millionaire. Many of the engines they built were still at work thirty years later; among these were George's Killingworth colliery engines. Throughout their lives they had perfect relations with all their workmen, even if George Stephenson did sometimes quarrel with his fellow engineers. He was familiar with his workmen, yet firm and fair, and they greatly respected him.

The two great men were able, in later life, to perform many generous and noble acts, too numerous to mention. Never, surely, have two great men achieved so much in the space of seventy-eight years, the time from George's birth in 1781 to Robert's death in 1859.

Date Chart

1781   George Stephenson born on 9th June at Wylam, Northumberland.
1789   Goes to work, as a cowherd at Dewley.
1791   Starts work at Dewley Burn colliery, as a picker.
1796   Made fireman at the Mid Mill Winning pit.
1799   Attends night school for the first time.
1802   Marries Frances Henderson.
1803   Birth of Robert, on 16th October.
1806   George's first wife dies of tuberculosis.
1812   Appointed engine-wright at Killingworth High pit.
1814   Builds his first locomotive, the *Blutcher*.
1815   Invents the "Geordie" safety lamp.
1820   Marries his second wife, Elizabeth Hindmarsh.
1822   Builds the Hetton Railway.
        Robert begins a course at Edinburgh University.
1823   George made chief engineer of the Stockton and Darlington Railway.
1824   Opens the locomotive works at Forth Street, Newcastle.
        Robert leaves England for South America.
1825   Opening of the Stockton and Darlington Railway.
1826   George appointed chief engineer of the Liverpool and Manchester Railway.
1827   Robert returns home from Colombia.
1829   The *Rocket* wins the locomotive trials at Rainhill.
        Robert marries Fanny Sanderson.

1830	Builds the Leicester and Swannington Railway.
	Opening of the Liverpool and Manchester Railway.
1833	Robert made chief engineer of the London and Birmingham Railway.
1838	Opening of the London and Birmingham Railway.
1845	George's second wife dies.
1846	Robert begins the High Level Bridge at Newcastle.
1848	George marries his third wife, Miss Gregory.
	George Stephenson dies on 12th August, aged 67.
1850	Robert's Britannia Bridge opened.
1859	Robert Stephenson dies on 12th October, aged 55.
1860	His Victoria Bridge opened by the Prince of Wales.
1862	George Stephenson's statue erected at Newcastle.

Glossary

Brakesman The man in charge of the winding engine at the head of a coal mine.

Bow and string girder A method of bridge building using long single arches to support the railway or road, giving the shape of a bow and string.

Box girder A hollow, square-shaped girder used in bridge building.

Colliery A coal mine; a deep shaft with a series of tunnels used for digging coal.

Engine-man The man in charge of a colliery engine.

Fire-damp Explosive hydrogen gas found in coal mines.

Fireman The man who starts up, or fires, a steam engine.

Geology The science dealing with the structure of the earth's crust, and the rocks on its surface.

Geordie Someone born on Tyneside.

Gig A light two-wheeled carriage drawn by a single horse.

Horse Power The power in an engine equal to the power of one horse.

Linesman An assistant to a surveyor, who surveys the lie of the land before the building of a road or railway.

Militia man A soldier drawn from civilian life, now called a conscript. It was possible to pay for a militia man to take your place in a war.

Perpetual Motion The motion of a machine which goes on for ever, driven by its own power. It is impossible to build such a machine.

Pleurisy A serious disease of the lungs.

Quick-silver The soft metal Mercury, which flows very easily, like water.

Safety lamp   A lamp with a protected flame used in coal mines, where a naked flame could cause an explosion.

Self-acting incline   A slope down which coal waggons run without being pulled by an engine.

Tuberculosis   A disease of the lungs common in the nineteenth century.

Tubular bridge   A bridge made of a long square tunnel through which the trains pass.

Viaduct   A long bridge with many arches for carrying a road or railway across a valley.

Further Reading

The best full length biography is *George and Robert Stephenson* by L. T. C. Rolt (Longman, 1960).

For a contemporary view, see *Lives of the Engineers* by Samuel Smiles (Vol. III, John Murray, 1862).

General histories of the railways are:

A History of British Railways by C. F. Dendy Marshall (Oxford University Press, 1938).

British Railway History 1836–1870 by C. Hamilton Ellis (Vol. I, Allen and Unwin, 1954).

Early Railways by J. B. Snell (Weidenfeld and Nicolson, 1964).

The Railways of Britain by Jack Simmons (Routledge and Kegan Paul, 1965).

North Western 1846–1922 by O. S. Nock (Ian Allan, 1968).

The London & North Western Railway by C. C. Dorman (Priory Press, 1975)

Index

Picture Credits

The author and publishers would like to thank all those who have given permission for their illustrations to appear on the following pages: Trustees of the British Museum: 8 (bottom); Victoria and Albert Museum: 33; Mary Evans Picture Library: 67; British Rail: 45, 60, 70, 82; Science Museum: *frontispiece*, title page, 9 (right), 11, 12, 18, 21, 22, 30, 38–39, 40–41, 41, 42, 46, 52–53, 54, 56–57, 62, 66, 69, 77, 78, 79, 86. The remaining pictures are the property of the Wayland Picture Library.